CLASSIC MOTORCYCLES

Norton

DON MORLEY

OSPREY
AUTOMOTIVE

Acknowledgements

Grateful thanks are due to the many Norton Owners' Club members who so kindly allowed me to photograph their beloved machines, to Alan Williams of the Imperial War Museum, also to Peter Thistle and Gladys Jones who helped with vital additional pictures.

Joy Emerson deserves a very special mention for patiently deciphering and typing my rather less-than-perfect manuscript, while thanks go to Nick Collins and Ian Penberthy of Osprey for their help, friendship and guidance. Bless them all for being pleasures to work with.

Don Morley
September 1990

Published in 1991 by Osprey Publishing
59 Grosvenor Street, London W1X 9DA

British Library Cataloguing in Publication Data

Morley, Don
    Norton.
    1. Norton motorcycles, history
    I. Title   II. Series
    629.2275
    ISBN 1-85532-140-8

Editor Ian Penberthy
Page design Janette Widdows
Printed in Hong Kong

Pic 55
Front cover
Tony Godfrey featuring in the first action colour shot I ever took, and on a production short-stroke Manx some time around 1955–6

Page 1
A 1959 Dominator 99 in the optional red colour scheme, and very nice it looks too

Page 2
A 1971 Commando Fastback — one of the best, in the author's view

Contents

Introduction

Older readers will know that despite Norton's domination of racing, their machines were comparatively rare sights on British roads, certainly until the early 1950s when this situation changed after tens of thousands of ex-War Department 16H models were sold off by the Army, or later still following the takeover by AMC and their resulting increased production of such models as the Dominator twins.

For most of the Bracebridge Street history, Norton were really but a tiny backwater company within a far greater industrial empire. Furthermore, with the latter's more profitable businesses including the supply of the (then) substantial tool kits for virtually every British motor car made, their motorcycle-producing offshoot was a relatively poor relation.

The Grand Prix and TT effort has often been blamed as distracting Norton from making and selling more or better roadsters, which overlooks the fact that, although the race team might well have been housed under the same factory roof, it also ran as yet another separate business. Given the team's world-beating and sustained success rate, they made a very considerable profit, too.

Mentioning this will, I hope, go some way to explaining, if not necessarily excusing, how one arm of any company could continue manufacturing for so long what, in Norton's instance, were often under-developed, staid and, indeed, downright stolid motorcycles, whereas at the same time, their other arm ruled the racing roost with exotica. (Many modern GP car and bike teams, remember, do not even bother manufacturing roadsters.)

The situation never existed where a Norton main dealer could boast of having a gleaming row of new machines all ready and available for immediate sale. Instead, it was a question of visiting the annual Motor Cycle Show and then ordering from a catalogue which, in turn, listed an apparently vast range of supposedly different models, all with separate code numbers and names.

Hence the humble ES2 was also a Chirk, and the otherwise identical twin-exhaust-pipe version, the Model 20, became the Kirby. Despite already having a name, the Model 30 and 40 Internationals were known as Clyde and Tenby respectively. All of these derivatives were accorded separate-model status for no other reason than their having slightly different handlebar bends, footrest positions, etc.

In this book, I have concentrated on Norton's main (or base) models for exactly such reasons. Furthermore, although those many other derivatives were listed, that did not necessarily mean that many, or even any, of them were actually manufactured, other than as show models. It merely meant that they could be ordered to that specification if the customer so wished.

Today's new Norton Motors Ltd, under Philippe Le Roux, recently managed a reverse takeover of the larger Minty Furnishing Group, which promised a collective annual turnover of £20 million. However, as I write, their shares are falling through the floor due to the poor economic situation, high interest rates and the latest Middle East crisis – we must hope that Norton are not dragged down again through no fault of their own.

Strange to ponder maybe, but the old NVT Group might still be alive and building conventional Trident-engined Commando derivatives were it not for their being crippled during the 1970s by Triumph's workers' sit-in. Meanwhile, the new company is being denied access to international Grand Prix racing's shop window, incredibly because the sport's governing body still can't decide whether rotarys are two- or four-strokes!

Above
This looks much like the works Brooklands racer 'Old Miracle', or 'Pa' Norton's own 1911 Isle of Man TT bike. Incredibly, though, this particular Model 9 is of 1920 vintage

Below
The 1939 single-exhaust-port 350 would have been a Model 50; this one has two ports, so it is a 55

Above

This Mk 3 Interstate Commando 850 of 1975 had covered over 100,000 miles in police hands before Paul Thomas acquired and restored it. The 850s were slower than the 750s because they never breathed quite as well

Right

Simon Buckmaster on Norton's new rotary at Ramsey Hairpin during 1988's TT races – they would be back in the thick of things by 1990

The making of a legend

At one time, Norton single-cylinder motorcycles dominated Grand Prix racing, winning virtually every 350 and 500 cc event, not once, but often year in and year out. Although their best days were over when the modern official World Championships were introduced (1949), this relatively tiny company still managed to win eight titles overall, to finish as runner-up on ten separate occasions, and to score 20 more third places.

Those impressive statistics, however, tell only a tiny part of the story, for they also scored 62 post-1949 World-Championship-counting Grand Prix wins along with 209 top-six places. Many, as in the instance of 1969's Yugoslav GP victory, were achieved literally years after the last racing Manx model left the factory.

For true road-racing enthusiasts, even those amazing achievements pale into insignificance when compared to Norton's amazing record of 38 wins in the Isle of Man TT. Remember, all were achieved with 350 and 500 cc engines, whereas it has taken the giant Japanese concerns nigh on 30 years of competing in every solo class to catch up.

Comparatively little is known about James Lansdown Norton who, of course, made it all possible. He was born in 1869 with an incurable heart disease and was not expected to live, yet he confounded the doctors by surviving. In time, he became a steam-engine model maker of considerable repute and then, in 1898, he set up a general engineering company in Birmingham bearing his name.

Norton joined the Royal Automobile Club in 1903, almost at the very moment when an unholy row broke out between the organization's two- and four-wheel members. The latter made a practice of crashing through the British police speed traps, whereas the slower motorcyclists usually got caught, thus costing the RAC more in legal representation fees.

The motorcyclists broke away to form the Auto Cycle Union, but the row had been bitter and public, causing Britain's government to decree that, in future, all motorized vehicles had to be officially registered and carry identifying numbers front and back, which would help the law enforcers trace and punish retrospectively any motorist who refused to stop.

No one in the British Isles had any real idea of how many motorized vehicles even existed prior to then. It may be of interest to record that there were 21,421 registered motorcycles by 1904 when these figures came in, and most used foreign engines.

Norton's contribution prior to 1907 would seem to be no more than a mere handful of machines, probably all built for himself or close friends and always using Belgian Clement or French Peugeot engines. However, he was — indeed, is — considered a founding father of Britain's motorcycle industry.

Meanwhile, the Auto Cycle Union had decided to hold the first ever Isle of

Norton's 1953 adverts publicizing their TT success still depicted Geoff Duke, although the Maestro had defected to Gileras by then. However, Ray Amm managed to win that year's Senior for Norton, and there would be another dozen such victories to come

Man TT race, the Marquis de Mouzilly St Mars' trophy being awarded to the fastest single rather than twin-cylinder machine, as the former were generally smaller engined and, therefore, considered to be at a slight disadvantage.

Horse-racing rules prevailed, with on-course betting and the riders weighing in like jockeys, and if necessary carrying extra ballast to bring them up to the stipulated minimum weight of 11 stone (154 lb). Fuel consumption was to be strictly rationed to emphasize further that the competing machines were indeed tourers, not racers (hence TT – Tourist Trophy).

The master plan was for each rider to cover $158\frac{1}{2}$ miles around an unmetalled, but fairly flat, triangular course, commencing at St Johns, then turning left at Ballacraine to follow the present-day mountain circuit as far as St Michaels village. Here, a very sharp left-hand hairpin headed them back along the Island's narrow coast road, via Peel, to the start area.

Rem Fowler's entry on his own Norton was a purely private venture like

Above
*Sammy Miller's superb museum houses
many priceless Nortons, including this
1905 Peugeot-engined 500 cc single,
which is the oldest known survivor*

Right
*Rem Fowler started the racing legend in
1907, with this very bike, by winning the
multi-cylinder class in the first ever TT
race*

most, but having been caught up in the great excitement generated by this pioneer event, 'Pa' Norton offered to go along as helper, and so witnessed the making of history.

In all, 25 riders started out in dry and very dusty conditions, with Matchless manufacturers Charlie and Harry Collier enjoying a real ding-dong dice in the single-cylinder class, and Fowler leading the twins ahead of Billy Wells' Vindec. All suffered numerous tumbles and a multitude of punctures.

Fowler set the fastest lap speed at a magnificent 42.91 mph and finished in 4 hours, 21.53 minutes overall, which was sufficient to win the twin-cylinder class, but was almost 12 minutes behind Charlie Collier's single. This was due in no small part to Rem becoming so exhausted that he pulled out to retire, only going on to win after a bystander mentioned that he was still almost half an hour ahead of Wells, his nearest rival.

Norton and TT racing have always seemed inseparable, but it was this first great win which really set the seal on the future. However, 'Pa' still only manufactured motorcycles occasionally and had no plans to even exhibit at 1907's end-of-year Motor Cycle Show. Indeed, had Moto Reve, the Peugeot engine importers, not volunteered to put Rem Fowler's bike on their stand, his marque might never have received wider acclaim.

The other side of Rem's 1907 winner

Pride before the fall

The weekly *Motor Cycle* magazine hardly danced up and down with excitement in 1908 by describing Norton's first annual show display as being 'small but interesting'. However, this was probably fair comment, for despite the stand logo shouting, 'My unapproachable Nortons', only two machines were featured, one being Fowler's already well-known and, by then, decidedly dated TT model.

The other bike's $3\frac{1}{2}$ hp, single-cylinder, side-valve did justify a little more attention, however, and not merely because it was the first of Norton's own make and design. It had a novel piston design with two oil-retaining grooves machined into the solitary compression ring, meaning that Norton invented the modern-day oil control ring.

Meanwhile, Norton achieved nothing for many a long year in the TT races and wrote bitter letters to the media, complaining that he alone was upholding the Tourist Trophy spirit, while his rivals were cheating. Furthermore, he castigated the increasing numbers of specially-designed, shorter-stroke or lighter-flywheel racing engines as being virtually evil!

His lone stand against progress took its biggest drubbing in 1911 when the TT moved to the present circuit. His and all other similar single-speed, belt-driven machines were going to have to make five climbs over the infamous Snaefell Mountain, at a time when the race organizers had also banned pedals.

Like most, Norton merely fitted a variable-speed, belt-drive-shaft pulley to his $3\frac{1}{2}$ hp engine and then chanced to luck. On the other hand, the American Hendee brothers, who built the Indian motorcycles, really entered into the spirit of things by sending over four chain-driven bikes with separate two-speed gearboxes.

The Hendee machines swept the board with an impressive 1-2-3 victory, the first ever by any foreign-made machine. This rout might have been greater still had their lone American rider, Jake de Rossier, not refuelled illegally and so been disqualified from an otherwise certain fourth place.

Never before had any single marque been so dominant or proved so reliable. Norton's effort ended, however, following unspecified mechanical problems suffered soon after completing his first lap and when he was lying in near to last place. Astonishingly, on his return to the mainland, he took out the following full-page advertisement:

'The American invasion, of distinctly American motorcycles, of distinctly American design, built for distinctly American conditions, should prove a warning to the wide awake Britishers. Machines manufactured abroad of foreign material and designed for service under different conditions never CAN be as reliable and efficient as a British built, made in England, of British material, by British workmen, designed for British service.'

World Speedway Champion Barry Briggs riding 1911's 'Old Miracle' on Brighton sea front at the conclusion of an early 1970s Pioneer Run

Sour grapes or merely misplaced patriotism, who knows? However, it spelt the end of an era, for less than six months later, he unveiled his first, unashamedly short-wheelbase, single-speed, 79 × 100 mm bore and stroke, side-valve-engined TT 490 cc Record Type. Although this out-and-out racer never would win a TT, such bikes took literally hundreds of world speed records at shorter circuits like Brooklands.

For instance, Jack Emerson bought one and rode it the 150 miles or so to that once famous banked track and promptly set seven new world records, including $73\frac{1}{2}$ mph for the mile, and 150 miles flat-out at an average of 64 mph. He then rode the bike another 150 miles back home, all in the same day.

By then, Norton was in dire financial trouble, however, following a serious recurrence of his lifelong illness. Even a move from the tiny Floodgate Street premises to an even smaller property in Sampson Road North failed to prevent him being declared bankrupt just before Christmas 1912.

Most of the bikes' components had been supplied and machined by the nearby toolmaking concern of R.T. (Bob) Shelley Ltd who, along with F. W. Lycett of saddle-making fame, suddenly found themselves not only 'Pa's' longest-standing friends, but also his largest creditors. This prompted Shelley to mount a rescue.

Far left

Tony Grantham's 1920 production Model 9 is virtually identical to 'Old Miracle', except for the variable-speed drive-belt pulley

Left

Outdated they may have been, but racing Model 9s, like Tony Grantham's, kept winning right into the 1920s because they were so spartan and light

The 16H was still a racer in 1922, which is when Dave Catton's fabulous outfit, featured here, was originally registered. Oh lucky man!

Shelley purchased what was left from the liquidators and invited 'Pa' to join with himself in the newly-constituted Norton Motors Ltd as joint managing director; C. A. Vandervell (later of CAV Automotive Electrical fame) was Chairman of both companies, while Bill Mansell was responsible for overseeing the new motorcycle business' day-to-day running.

'Mr. Bill', as Mansell became known throughout Britain's motorcycle industry, proved himself to be a real visionary. Although it was already too late to mount an official effort in 1913's Isle of Man races, he determined that they should enter a full three-man works team for the following year (Norton's first ever team entry).

Not that 1914's effort would prove successful, for one bike retired, while brothers O. G. and R. J. P. Brand, riding the other two, finished in 46th and

Victor Horsman successfully raced this works 16H at Brooklands in 1919. The new model number for what was much the same old bike was due to the fitment of a clutch and three-speed gearbox

51st places. However, at least Norton were back. The non-finishing third man happened to be a certain D. O'Donovan, who was one of the most famous Brooklands track racing devotees, and R. T. Shelley's brother-in-law.

This close family liaison had already resulted in the Brooklands Special (BS) Racer, itself a variation of the older TT 490 cc Record Type, and would go on to foster the better-equipped (with brakes!) Brooklands Road Special (BRS). Eventually, it would result in Norton's similarly-engined range of racing and roadster 16Hs (i.e. same again, but with chain drive and a gearbox).

Every BS Racer came with a certificate stating that its engine had already been tested by O'Donovan at Brooklands and at a minimum of 75 mph over a timed flying kilometre. However, there was one particularly frustrating period when not a single engine reached anything like this speed, despite 'Old

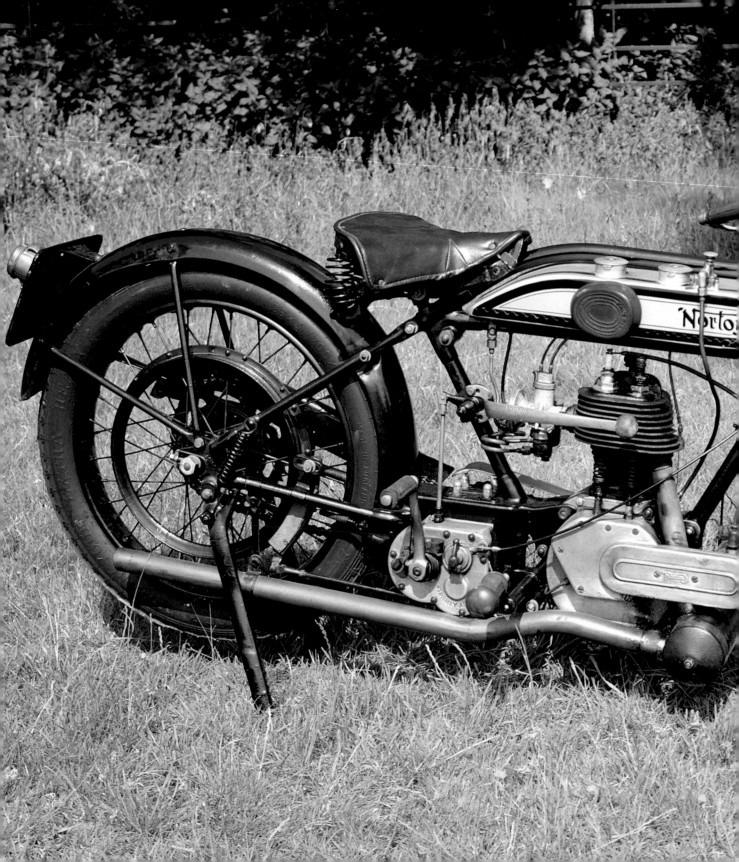

Tony Johnson's solo 16H of 1924 might appear to mirror Dave Catton's machine, but a closer look reveals expanding-hub brakes for what, by then, had become a Sports Tourer

Miracle' (the test rig bike) being swooped down off the top of Brooklands 1 in 1 banking.

Further frantic tests revealed that the supposed racers were actually slower than their untuned roadster counterparts, causing quite a panic back at the factory. Then someone remembered that they had begun using a new and smoother-finished cylinder/cylinder head casting mould at the same time that they had experienced the sudden loss of power.

Not a great deal was known about engine tuning in those days, so Norton's personnel could be excused for not realizing that the earlier, rougher castings created exactly the right degree of gas turbulence needed to give those engines their ultimate turn of speed.

The old moulds were rescued from the factory scrap heap once that penny had dropped, and O'Donovan went on to set over a hundred further world speed records with the side-valvers, including raising the flying kilometre to an astonishing 82.85 mph in 1915, at a time when many of his compatriots were fighting a world war.

Ed Duck's machine still shows a strong family resemblance to 'Old Miracle', but it is a 1937 version which had put on surplus weight

Dougie Brown very nearly gave the 16H a Senior TT win in 1920, but despite leading handsomely into the last lap, he lost out because his pit crew gave him an ill-advised 'Slow down and save the engine' signal. He slowed just a little too much, allowing Tommy De La Hay to win on a Sunbeam.

The 16H, or 'big four', side-valvers, and their numerous derivatives, were demoted to a touring role by 1923, following the introduction of the ohv engine. However, they lived on to see active service during World War 2 before increasing obsolescence, and middle-aged spread, finally killed them off in 1954.

The other side of Ed's 1937 16H which, incidentally, has been re-registered. I am none too sure that the electric horn was fitted originally

Valves moved upstairs

Until 1920, and up to the time of the move to larger premises in Bracebridge Street, Norton had only ever manufactured relatively simple 500 cc, or larger, side-valve engines of near identical design. They differed from each other in little more than mere detail and the cylinder bore size or piston's length of stroke.

A long-stroke configuration had been settled on, with dimensions of 79×100 mm for all 500 cc engines (actually 490 cc) and 82×120 mm on such as the 633.7 cc side-valve 'big four' (give or take a few prototypes). Those same dimensions would live along with most bottom-half engine components in the coming ohv and ohc powerplants.

Therefore, 1922's prototype ohv Model 18 racer engine was based on a mildly-modified 16H side-valve bottom end, but fitted with a new cylinder barrel and head, crowned with a rocker box that was linked by a pair of long pushrods. The new bike's main frame received a stirrup-shaped bend in the top tube to clear this taller engine.

Brooklands ace Don O'Donovan was given the job of testing this prototype, but he declared that he was not overly impressed, until it was clocked at 98 mph, appreciably faster than his beloved side-valve racer 'Old Miracle'. Consequently, Norton lost little time in introducing the production models for the coming racing season.

Graham Black very nearly won 1923's Senior TT, the resulting bike's first major outing, although eventually he finished $1\frac{1}{2}$ minutes behind Tim Sheard's winning Douglas. Whereas the latter had enjoyed a trouble-free ride, Black had crashed and then lost several vital minutes in making repairs, so this result might easily have been reversed.

Fortunately, Black managed to finish second. Graham Walker (Murray's father) managed fourth, Tommy Simister fifth, and Jimmy Shaw sixth, giving Norton the almost as prestigious manufacturer's team prize. Walker also finished second with Tucker third on similar bikes in that week's Sidecar TT.

Alec Bennett finally laid Norton's 'nearly year' ghost by winning 1924's Senior at a shattering 61.64 mph, which was a faster average than the previous best ever single lap time. George Tucker similarly made amends by winning the sidecar race with Walter Moore, the company's new chief development engineer, appropriately riding shotgun.

About the only thing these 1924 bikes did not win was the TT's Team Prize, for Joe Craig crashed. However, he made up for it later by becoming one of Norton's directors, and their longest standing, most successful racing manager ever. Ironically, he also became infamous for never forgiving anyone who dared fall off one of HIS precious machines.

All but the works-racer-type, four-speed gearboxes became standard equipment for the 1926 over-the-counter models, when the 588 cc Model 19

Left
Vast numbers of 16Hs saw military service in every theatre of World War 2

sidecar racing engine also went public, as this class allowed engines of up to 600 cc. Thus, Norton repeated their side-valve-to-ohv conversion exercise, but with a 'big four' rather than 16H bottom end.

Stanley Woods' works-entered Model 18 easily won 1926's Senior TT at another all-time record of 67.54 mph. These machines continued as Norton's Grand Prix racers until the following year, when Walter Moore unveiled his overhead-cam engine. In typical Norton fashion, this closed the door on any further ohv model development.

The Model 18, 19 and ES2 engines were all allowed to stagnate from then onwards, as the bikes they powered became increasingly stodgy and

Above

Bert Denley and his ohv Model 18, after winning 1923's 200-mile race at Brooklands. Don O'Donovan is standing behind (smoking a pipe)

Left

A genuine Model 19 Brooklands Racer of 1926, and what is more, a one-owner unrestored machine at that

overweight tourers. The final 1940s and 1950s versions, with their telescopic front forks and rear suspensions, gave no clue of any past racing history.

Having owned and covered thousands of miles on such machines, stemming from several different eras, my own view is that the 1920s bikes were quite the finest handling, fastest, and most rideable of the entire flat-tank period, especially those built between 1927 and 1929. They alone enjoyed the benefit of an 8 in. front brake which was essential to contain so much usable performance.

Acceleration to 70 mph compares well with modern, big single trail bikes, not least because the comparatively flimsy Norton has an appreciably better power-to-weight ratio. Indeed, mine used to win most traffic light GPs against all-comers on its many working trips across London during the 1980s.

The enclosed-pushrod, three-speed, saddle-tank jobs of 1930 were almost as quick, but from then on, these bikes became ever heavier without any matching increases in engine power. Even so, the ultra-heavy, penultimate

Showing the patina of age and, hopefully, far too nice to restore, the other side of the Brooklands 600 cc racer

18s, 19s and plunger ES2s are surprisingly pleasant to ride, that is provided one is happy to plod around at a leisurely 45–50 mph.

Riding impressions of the final and fantastic-handling Featherbed ES2 and 350 cc Model 50 are, if anything, a little harder to summarize. Although far lighter than their immediate predecessors, they suffer from frustratingly slow engines housed in a race-developed chassis, which could be likened to putting up with a Mini engine in a Ferrari.

A superbly-restored 1925 Model 18 racer being belted through Ballacraine on the TT course by Keith Shorrock

Above right

April 1928, and H. J. Bacon, seen here with his very early production ES2, has just won at Brooklands at 88.08 mph. The full-cradle, triple-rear-stay frame, rear-mounted magneto, etc, are all standard

Below right

CS1-type saddle tanks, and beginning to put on flab – that just about sums up Norton's 1930 models, such as this Model 18

Far right

The other side of the same 1930 Model 18, showing the rather beautiful cast-aluminium primary chain cover. Unfortunately, it was only a cover and could not hold oil

Left
*Norton's later 1930s ohv engine revamp
brought in converging pushrod tubes, and
rear-mounted magnetos for all*

Below
*Roy Jeanes' Model 55 twin-port 350 of
1937, showing the later two-part, pressed-
tin primary chaincase. This lasted until
the Commando, but still rarely held oil*

Overleaf
*'Heavy and sluggish' are the words that
come to mind when describing the tele-
fork, plunger-rear-suspension ES2
models. However, Roger Deadman, who
owns this beautifully-restored 1951
version, might not agree*

Above

A larger-capacity, swinging-rear-fork 19S of 1956 – longer, even heavier, but certainly offering far better handling than any of the 'garden gate' versions

Right

Most riders cried out for more power than the likes of this 1958 wideline Featherbed Model 50 could ever give. However, the 350 cc engines were much smoother than the 500s

*Freer-revving and less prone to chronic
vibration than the equivalent ES2, in
some ways, the 350 was nicest of the two*

Most UK-bound slimline Featherbeds went to the Royal Automobile Club for patrol duty. Indeed, that was the fate of this 1962 example, now owned by Norton Owners' Club member Tony Johnson

Camshafts on loan

Norton's race team were passing through a lean period by 1923, despite being equipped with very powerful ohv engines, or rather because of them. Those engines were becoming too powerful for the, by then, long outdated and severely under-braked chassis.

The real problem was one of haphazard development (most British motorcycles suffered this syndrome regardless of era), so Norton called in Walter Moore to put matters right. Apart from being an ex-TT rider himself, he had also been responsible for much of the rival Douglas concern's engineering and development.

Moore lost little time in giving Norton's roadsters and racers such essential items as better lubrication and brakes. Then, he turned his hand to designing a full-cradle frame to replace the previous open version, which used to bend in the middle whenever the engine's considerable power was used to the full.

This is the point at which Norton's racers began to grow apart from the roadsters, the cradle-framed 500 becoming the new, racing-only, Model ES2. On the other hand, the previous racing 18 kept the same basic engine, but never did get a cradle. It continued onwards into the mid 1950s, reduced to the role of a humble, and increasingly heavyweight, tourer.

Then followed one of the most unusual sequences of events in the history of the British motorcycle industry, for in his spare time, and whilst working from home, Moore devised a simple overhead-camshaft conversion for Norton's ohv engine. This his employer accepted without making him any extra payment, fitting it more or less straight into their Moore-designed ES2 chassis.

Unveiled as it was in May 1927, there was just time to rush three CS1 (camshaft one) machines to the magic Island for the beginning of TT practice. There, Stanley Woods and Alec Bennett cannily completed parts of the course on them at high speeds, but toured round elsewhere to fox the opposition, leaving Joe Craig as the only CS1 rider putting in any rapid complete laps.

Craig's best practice speed of 69.1 mph almost gave the team's game away, for the lap time was only 48 seconds off the circuit's absolute record. However, in the race itself, his bike proved difficult to start, so it was left to Stanley Woods, whose speed was 70.50 mph for the first lap, to show this engine's true capabilities. Remember, this all-time record best speed was from a standing start.

Woods piled on the pressure, holding a massive four minutes lead over his team-mate Bennett by the end of lap four, with Craig fighting his way up to 12th place. Then a murmur of sympathy rustled around the course as reports came in of Stanley retiring with clutch trouble, which left Bennett to win easily at a new record 68.41 mph race average.

Later in the year, Woods certainly made up for this disappointment by winning the Belgian, Dutch and Swiss GPs, and gaining second places in two others. Percy (Tim) Hunt, similarly mounted on a CS1, easily won both 1927's and 1928's Amateur TTs. On the latter occasion, he also shattered the circuit's outright speed record (TT and MGP) by lapping at 71.05 mph.

Arguably, much of this sudden spate of success could be attributed to Moore's introduction of decent brakes and the new cradle frame, rather than merely any extra power from his engine. After all, this was still basically a modified ES2 unit with a new offside crankcase half casting to accept the simple internal, rather than external, oil pump and, of course, bevel gears to drive that overhead cam.

Those bottom bevels drove a long vertical shaft that ran past the virtually standard ES2 cylinder barrel (with slight fin shape differences) up to a pair of matching top bevels driving a single camshaft high aloft. Indeed, even the cylinder head was basically ES2, although it had only one set of indents for the vertical drive, rather than two as required by pushrods.

Likewise, cam profiles were much as in the cooking engines, but, unlike previous Norton practice, the magneto drive was taken directly from this (and the ES2) engine's drive-shaft-side main sprocket (as the dynamo drive on later AMC singles). The magneto itself was moved from the front to a rear mounting platform on the opposite side.

This latter facet made these powerplants look deceptively tall, and led to their popular 'cricket bat' nickname. With none of the normal auxiliaries

Eleven-times TT winner Stanley Woods poses on his works bike in 1926. It is not a 'cammy' model yet, however, although it does display what would soon be the new CS1's petrol and oil tanks, etc

STANLEY WOODS "NORTON" 1926 T.T. RACES

mounted on the offside in the usual manner, the actual overhead-camshaft components looked remarkably uncluttered and, indeed, of cricket bat shape.

For 1928's racing season, Moore unveiled his scaled-down 350 cc versions of the CS1 and the pushrod engines, the first time, incidentally, that Norton had ever produced any machine of less than 500 cc capacity. Then, he received a staggering inducement to take his designs to Germany and become NSU's new development chief.

The offer reputedly exceeded £75,000 per annum (a figure neither denied nor confirmed in later interviews with the man himself) and was made by a company enjoying a near bottomless budget that was intent on taking up racing and moving straight in at the top level. Moore remained happily at Norton, however, declining to move on several occasions.

NSU finally suggested that he named his own figure, and later he did admit to mentioning an amount so astronomical that he was convinced it would get them off his back, yet pay it they did. Hence, Walter found himself en route to Germany in mid 1929, carrying his CS1 engine drawings for NSU's use, and leaving Norton without a replacement ohc engine to race.

Left
Photographed at Brooklands shortly after I rebuilt it, my own 1927 CS1

Below
Sorry about the surplus holes in the primary chaincase, which I really should have welded up. It is interesting to speculate that my old bike must surely have been a one-time works racer, not least because the production jobs did not arrive until 1928

International glory

Shortly after Walter Moore's departure, Norton's 1929 works team appeared with a visibly different ohc engine, which had been hurriedly designed for the remainder of the season by his replacement, Arthur Carroll. However, this was not yet the International as we now know it, rather a mixture of that eventual engine's bottom end and the earlier type upper half.

These engines were actually stop-gap measures devised to get around his predecessor's patents. As they were housed in Moore's ES2 chassis, they also continued with his CS1 (500 cc) and CJ (350 cc) model designations, although there were few visual similarities, either to past versions or future ones, and none was made for sale.

What tends to confuse with these ultra-rare, ES2-frame-and-fuel-tank C models is that they finally entered limited production after December 1931 and the true International's arrival. However, they were low-state-of-tune, ohc trials bikes with parallel, as opposed to downdraught, cylinder head inlet ports. The completely redesigned 'Inter', on the other hand, instantly assumed the road-racing role.

Carroll obviously took a leaf out of Velocette's book when completing the redesign, for the similarities between the International's internal parts and those of Velocette's racing K series were far too numerous to have been purely coincidental. However, he failed to learn from, or did not dare to take a good enough look at, the K's infinitely superior upper cam box, which retained its lubricant, something his rarely did.

His complete International transformation of the ohc Models 30 (500 cc) and 40 (350 cc) for 1930's works TT racers included new frames, downdraught cylinder heads and those redesigned cam boxes. Even so, Norton were still beaten by Rudge that year, although they were far better sorted for 1931 when they scored the first of many subsequent Junior/Senior double victories.

Internationals, or Inters as they are far more popularly known, finished a resounding 1-2-3 in 1931's Senior and took the first two Junior race places. In 1932, they were fitted with experimental front fork check-springs and not only managed a 1-2-3 in both capacity classes, but also won September's 'Manx' and ten straight Continental GPs in a row.

Lack of space precludes further statistics of what became Norton's glory years, when those immortal Inters earned and maintained their name with near total domination of racetracks world-wide. Remarkably, they were much as anyone could go out and buy, for what was works-only specification one year, usually became generally available to all in the next.

Works team bike goodies, such as fork check springs and hairpin valve operation for instance, became standard on all machines for 1934, and each Inter came supplied with full road equipment right up until 1936, when Norton finally offered a separate model that was already stripped for action.

This marked the point at which the true racing Inters began to grow away from those bought entirely as roadsters.

There would be little further development of any real significance on the touring models from then onwards, other than the post-war adoption of alloy instead of cast-iron cylinder heads and barrels, which were optional for the 'garden gate' models and standard on the final Featherbeds. Incidentally, the latter scored Norton's last Clubman's TT 1-2-3 victory before BSA muscled in with their own all conquering Gold Stars.

Chassis changes were always minimal, with such as plunger suspension becoming an optional extra for 1937, then being standardized post-war when telescopic Roadholder front forks also took over from the previous girders. However, not much else was altered until the arrival of those alloy engines and the production Featherbed frames in 1952 for 1953's models.

Norton's all-conquering International even featured on this mid-1930s Isle of Man postcard; today, it would probably be a Honda!

A SENIOR T.T. WINNER

Meanwhile, the racing versions grew almost totally apart, being given, among other things, improved cam-box oiling systems, hotter cams, lighter flywheels, higher piston compression ratios, larger-capacity fuel and oil tanks, special tuning (costing £5 extra from 1936), larger-bore carburettors, BTH racing magnetos and alloy top ends. All of these items arrived prior to the war.

One popular misconception, often repeated by today's media, is that these pre-1939, over-the-counter, racing Internationals were, in fact, Manxes. This was certainly not the case, for neither Norton nor anyone else ever used that particular name until after 1946. However, it is admittedly an abbreviation of the name given in 1939 to six special prototypes.

The official works racing team had been disbanded by then, and Norton

Left

Where are you now DKP 748? For many years, this 1937 Model 40 belonged to me. I have to admit, though, that I took the easy route with the fuel and oil tanks' restoration!

Far left

A superbly-restored Model 40 (350) of 1936, complete with the correct T-shaped battery and partially-chromed petrol and oil tanks, all exactly as should be

Not strictly original, but who cares? Like most genuine late-1930s racing Inters, this one has been updated over the years

production had been switched entirely to building side-valve 16Hs in readiness for the inevitable war, but not before half-a-dozen officially titled 'Manx Grand Prix' models had been built. These were loaned to a few fancied privateers who, it was hoped, would keep Bracebridge Street's racing flag flying.

Those 1940 pre-production models were not wheeled out again until 1947, when they appeared with telescopic front forks instead of girders. This was when the production racer's name was shortened to 'the Manx'. Naturally enough, they carried on winning as before.

A *Motor Cycle* magazine staff man once enjoyed a brief canter on Stanley

The only known surviving Manx Grand Prix Model of 1939, taken just after it had been restored by its lucky owner, John Flood. Incidentally, note the correct forward-folding rear stand

Woods' 1934 TT winner and waxed lyrical, although he said little of real consequence, whereas the only other Inter test that I can recall came 43 years later, when *Motor Cycling* just managed to squeeze 97 mph out of a 1947 bike. This had been fitted with race cams and a Brooklands track silencer that was guaranteed to release extra power.

Such an incredible gap, or apparent lack of interest, could not possibly happen nowadays, but the press of that era sadly colluded with Britain's then all-powerful motorcycle industry in making sure that such grand illusions were rarely, if ever, tested. Therefore, having owned and covered many thousands of miles on more than a dozen such racers and roadsters myself,

Above
Harley Deschamps, seen here on John Flood's MGP Model, was its actual rider in that 1939 Junior TT. His horrendous second-lap crash at Quarry Bends and subsequent long hospitalization saw to it that both he and the bike were still in the Island by the start of World War 2. This was largely responsible for assuring the machine's eventual survival

Right
Close-up of another late-1930s racing International's engine department. But for the girder front forks, instead of telescopics, this machine might well be a post-war period Manx

maybe a few additional comments might not go amiss.

Fastest and best handling, in my experience, were the very early and final alloy-engined Featherbed versions, for these alone enjoy appreciably lighter cycle components along with stiffer main frames. Thus, they offer superior power-to-weight ratios coupled to more positive hairline steering, a good 1932 or 1957 half-litre machine being capable of topping the ton without resorting to racing extras

All of the early rigids handle particularly well because their centre of gravity lies very low in relation to the ground. Plunger rear suspension, on the other hand, especially if combined with tele forks, raises this level, adding considerably to the overall weight to ruin the entire equation. Indeed, all similarly-equipped Inters suffer from stodgy and decidedly unsporting handling.

Rigid and Featherbed 350s should top 90 mph reasonably easily (at least, according to 'Mr Smith' and his speedometers). As both sizes of engine are wonderfully free-revving with oodles of usable torque, neither needs the standard-fitment, close-ratio gear set. Therefore, I have always found it better

Pre-war Inters won the Manx Grand Prix amateur races on literally dozens of occasions, and the post-war Clubman's TT another six times. Those machines included the likes of this beautiful-looking, but ultra-heavy and evil-handling, 'garden gate' Model 30 of 1949

to substitute a wider-ratio ES2 gear set, which is less of a pain to use on today's roads.

Rebuilding a Model 30 or 40 engine need hold no great terrors either, for they are remarkably simple. Indeed, they are much as Model 18s and ES2s, with a few extra, but minor, complications, like a need to shim the upper and lower bevel gears to obtain perfect mesh. Some of these engines' ball and roller bearings are no longer obtainable which, eventually, will mean remachining bearing housings or shafts to accept modern bearing size equivalents. Beyond this, however, there is little to worry about, given a source of shims, some common sense and a modicum of patience, which are all needed for assembling, dismantling and reassembling the bevel gear housings as often as it takes until the clearances are right.

Left

Not the Clubman's, but 1960's full International Senior TT, in readiness for which, Roly Capner (no. 45) tickles the carburettor of his Featherbed Model 30 on the start line

Below

Late 1980s in the Isle of Man, and a momentary pause for what then was my 1959 Model 30. It was being used at the time for learning the TT course during practice week by modern day racer Stu Avant from New Zealand. He much appreciated the Manx brakes, which had been fitted from new by Norton as optional extras

Norton's traditional black and silver
finish was optional for the Model 30 and
40. Personally, I much prefer the
standard metallic silver-grey, as on this
1955–6 beauty. Few people realize that
Inter oil and fuel tanks were of larger
capacity than the Dominator equivalents

Everyone's racer

The book has not been written yet detailing how Norton's fabulous Manx racers steadily evolved during more than three decades. When, or rather if, someone does undertake such a monumental task, then merely cataloguing the veritable multitude of annual modifications will take far more words than are available for my modest offering.

Further complicating matters is the fact that these Manxes also enjoyed a ten- or 20-year competitive lifespan, often suffering horrendous blow-ups, major crashes, and many subsequent rebuilds in the process, not to mention regular mechanical updates from the period's specialist tuners. As a result, there is virtually no such animal as a standard Manx Norton.

The late-1930s-onwards works team bikes also grew ever further away from what could be bought, with, for instance, short- rather than long-stroke engines, double overhead camshafts; and copies of BMW telescopic front forks arriving pre-war. The ordinary production engines remained long-strokes until the mid 1950s, by which time, Joe Craig's factory specials had already taken more quantum leaps.

Craig's taciturn reputation remains unparalleled in motorcycle racing's entire history, and his power at Norton was such that when Bert Hopwood,

Actually a late-1948 'garden gate' Manx, but it might have been a 1940 model had the war not intervened

Above

An assembly of talent! Riders Johnny Lockett (no. 42), Ken Bills (no. 1) and Harold Daniell (no. 14) after finishing second, fourth and first respectively in 1949's Senior TT. At far left is Rex McCandless, later of Featherbed fame. Also included are the famous tuner Steve Lancefield, Gilbert Smith, Norton's then managing director (between bikes 42 and 1), and the wizard himself, Joe Craig (between Daniell and Bills)

Right

Daytona was still a mixed road and sand race in 1950, so Norton fitted roadster-type tin primary chaincases to their all-conquering double-ohc works Manxes. They also had International bottom gear ratios plus a kick starter, primarily lest any of their riders should stall

their chief designer, paid Joe's engine test-bed facility a courtesy visit, he was told he could not enter and had the door slammed firmly in his face! (I even managed to get kicked out of the garden of Craig's 1954 TT race headquarters for merely chatting to rider Ray Amm, who happened to be a personal friend.)

Despite the many well-known stories about Joe's oft-brutish behaviour, he was most certainly a brilliant engineer, talent spotter and also racing tactician. Every year, he managed to squeeze a little more horsepower from his beloved, yet already venerable, singles, and at ever higher revs without any resulting loss of reliability.

At Norton, he remained literally a law unto himself, being respected grudgingly, while his behaviour was tolerated because he brought them more

Above

Geoff Duke on his 1952 World Championship-winning, outside-flywheel, Joe Craig bike during an indecently-fast mid-1980s TT lap of honour. The Maestro showed that he had lost little of his previous finesse

Left

This was what 'Joe Public' got for 1953 – dohc, but still long-stroke. This is my own 500 cc Manx of many years ago, mid rebuild and all correct, including the high, swan-necked, clip-on handlebars

Far left

Craig's 1952–4 outside-flywheel Manxes fairly bristled with non-standard innovations, including a frame-mounted oil cooler and massive front engine breather assembly. The bits that really matter, however, are hidden inside

Above right
Ray Amm practised on this fully-streamlined works 'kneeler' for 1953's North West 200, but chose a conventional bike for the race

Below right
Laying the engine down resulted in a rather long powerplant, so Craig also devised an interesting semi-unit-construction gearbox for this non-Featherbed-framed bike. This allowed the wheelbase to be kept at the desired size

Far right
Craig's Moto-Guzzi-inspired, outside-flywheel, laid-down-engine Manx of 1953–4, pictured after its later rescue and superb restoration by Sammy Miller

The late, great, John Hartle with the very last of Joe Craig's bikes at the weigh-in for 1954's Junior TT and, gentleman that he was, posing for the author's then humble box camera

fame and fortune than they really deserved. His machines' incredible success rate prompted the chain, oil, spark plug, circuit, petrol and tyre companies to queue up with sponsorship money, which put Norton's team in profit before a bike turned a wheel, and without counting winnings.

Craig's life ended, however, in a horrific car crash in March 1957, just weeks after his retirement. Sadly, he never confided his tuning secrets, or passed on any notes, although some very special works engines and individual components surfaced years later when the parent AMC company were eventually bankrupted. (By then, however, no one knew the original development purpose or thinking behind them.)

The Manx models' more obvious highlights include Rex McCandless and Arthur (Artie) Bell's Featherbed frame design which, incidentally, stemmed from entirely private experiments during 1944. The result was offered to BSA first, but incredibly they said that they were not interested. Then, there were 1953–4's all-conquering, outside-flywheel works engines, for which Craig had taken a leaf out of Moto Guzzi's book, using a very light, bobweight-type crankshaft to reduce oil drag.

These engines, in particular, led to 1953's fully-streamlined and phenomenally fast 'kneeler' machines, as used in practice for the TT and North West 200 events, but they were not actually raced. They also paved the way for 1956's unfaired, but equally Moto Guzzi-inspired, five-speed, laid-flat engine version. For reasons we shall now probably never know, this likewise was held in reserve.

Craig reverted to the pre-war works semi-short-stroke 90 × 78.4 mm

Left

Norton's former works star, John Surtees, at Brands Hatch – not a period picture, however, for this was taken during an early 1980s Classic race

Below

Geoff Duke's own experimental Norton for 1957 featured a Reynolds-built, ultra-light, oil-carrying frame with leading-link forks. He won on it second time out, although there was never enough money available to develop it properly

Right
*Derek Minter was the 'King of Brands' on
Bill Lacey-tuned Nortons*

Far right
*One of Doug Hele's final few production
development Manxes which, incidentally,
were faster than Joe Craig's earlier works
exotica*

Below
*Not even 'Banbury Dan' Shorey's 'Peel
Mountain Mile' full fairing would give
his Senior TT Manx sufficient extra
speed to stay with the dominant MVs,
Hondas, and Yamahas by 1965, although
he still finished 16th*

Roger Munsey showing a clean pair of heels to all comers in the 1983 Classic Race at Brands Hatch, and on a slightly tatty, but remarkably standard-looking, 500 cc Manx

(500 cc) dimensions, and 78 × 73 mm for the 350 outside-flywheel jobs, to gain extra torque. This period's heavier, internal-flywheeled production Manxes, however, adopted the virtually square configuration of 86 × 85.6 mm and 76 × 76.7 mm respectively.

Works engine output figures were never released, but reliable period sources reckoned that the 500s enjoyed a genuine 50 bhp at the rear wheel. The production equivalents rarely bettered 48.5 bhp, and only then when measured from the crankshaft and at 7000 rpm, which was also some 600 rpm slower (beyond which revs power delivery rapidly tailed off).

Featherbed frames graced the production Manx from September 1951, and a dual-leading-shoe front brake arrived for 1953, while AMC's infinitely superior gearboxes came along a couple of years later. Post-Joe Craig development shot forward under Doug Hele, with Bert Hopwood's guidance. This included 1959–60's desmodromic and rotary-valve experiments which, though promising, failed to reach fruition.

Some 250 Manxes were built and sold during 1959 (appreciably more than in any other year), while 1960 brought another prototype 'low boy', as raced successfully by both John Hartle and Geoff Duke. Then 1961's major revamp introduced the double-sided, twin-leading-shoe front brake, higher compression ratios, considerable changes to the bevel-drive-shaft arrangement, larger Amal GP2 carburettors, and rubber-band-mounted oil tanks. Popular opinion among some of the more famous tuning exponents is that the 1959-series engines were actually best, although the late, great, Reg Deardon always claimed to prefer the long-stroke engines' greater torque, certainly for Isle of Man racing. He reckoned that this factor alone gave his runners the benefit of several vital seconds shaved from every lap whilst the bikes were climbing the mountain.

The long-strokes undoubtedly enjoyed wider powerbands, along with fantastic reliability, whereas the higher-revving short-strokes allowed those revs to be sustained. However, this was at the expense of a noticeable loss of flexibility due to increased 'megaphonitis', and more piston and gudgeon-pin failures, which generally wrecked a powerplant's entire upper half.

Rebuilding these engines was never particularly difficult, although obviously, it takes a real expert to extract every last drop of available power. Manxes are perfectly tractable as roadsters, too, provided they are given slightly less tall gearing, a compression lowering plate, a silencer, etc (my two were used in this way for several years after their racing heyday).

However, many original components are cast in magnesium (electron), which reacts badly to the corrosive elements in the air and suffers stress fractures rather too easily. Consequently, items like brake plates and wheel hubs in particular need frequent regular safety inspections, not least because most will have been crashed more than once, so they may already be cracked and potentially lethal.

Reliability trials

Jack Williams won the Scottish Six Days twice when he, George Holdsworth, Vic Brittain, Graham Goodman and Norton's two greatest sidecar aces, Dennis K. Mansell and Harold Flook, collectively saw to it that Bracebridge Street's off-road team were just about as dominant between the world wars as their road-racing colleagues.

Incidentally, that era's factory trials bikes were almost invariably the overhead-cam CJ (350s) or CS1 (500s), which enjoyed little more than $3\frac{1}{2}$ in. of hummock-bashing ground clearance, yet this failed to concern either Graham Goodman, who put up 1931's best up-to-350 cc performance, or Jack Williams three years later when he won the rock-strewn Highlands Classic overall.

Any pre-1940s Norton model could be ordered ready fitted with trials tyres, wide-ratio gears, high-level exhaust system and, with the Inter's exception, a minimally-higher-ground-clearance (export Colonial type) frame. Collectively, this competition trim cost a not inconsiderable £5 extra.

Norton amended this practice post-war by merely offering a single, telescopic-front-fork, ohv Model 18 trials version copied from Jack Williams' 1937 Scottish Six Days winner. However, this bike rapidly proved itself too long, low and heavy for the later period's prevailing conditions, especially when compared to such machines as the rival AMC concern's nippier 350s.

Meanwhile, the famous road-racing McCandless brothers of Ulster, and similarly Ray Petty in England, fitted military-model 16H main frames to their own private trials bikes, as this happened to lop 3 in. off the Model 18's over-long wheelbase and also saved considerable weight. Norton's own works team, however, were soldiering on with the genuine item.

Why Bracebridge Street's own boffins never thought of this dodge has always been a bit of a mystery, but once they had been given the idea on a plate, they lost little more time in copying it, unveiling what became the new 500T. However, those occasional trials-riding road-racers who first thought of the idea received very little in the way of thanks.

Only the front fork yolks, fuel tank, footrests, front brake plate, Dunlop rubber saddle, wider handlebars, smaller steering damper knob, sump shield, exhaust system and shorter kickstart shaft were actually unique to this brilliant parts-bin machine. The remaining 98 per cent of components came directly from various other models.

There were additional detail modifications, however, including re-siting the 16H-type oil tank's filler from side entry to the top, and minor alterations to the frame/fuel tank fitting lugs to slim the ensemble down slightly. The engine remained the standard ES2/Model 18 unit until 1950, when Wellworthy's alloy cylinder barrel replaced the latter's cast-iron component.

Many a rider first found fame on these lightweight bikes which had brilliant handling, but perhaps none more so than multi World Road Racing

Champion Geoff Duke who, in his earlier days as a Norton trials team member, earned off-road immortality with his unequalled feat of winning 1950's Victory Trial without losing a single mark.

Likewise, my own very minor competitive career began with just such a Norton, which was trialed, scrambled, grass-tracked and, on one occasion, even road-raced, quite apart from carrying me daily to and from work. It hardly ever seemed to require any maintenance, beyond the occasional change of oil, tyres or chains.

Norton quietly killed off the 500T at the end of 1953 rather than provide it with a much-needed rear-sprung frame. Although a sad event, it was perhaps also wise, for the long-stroke engines were always at their happiest when pulling a very tall gear and firing once every couple of lamp posts, which by the mid 1950s was no longer a great asset.

Riding one again in a trial recently certainly suggested this to be true, for sections even in classic trials nowadays require snap power and instant acceleration, rather than heavy-flywheeled, stump-pulling 'plonk'. The 500T felt positively 'wheezy' and no longer up to the job.

The author's 1949 Model 500T, photographed many years ago when it was still original, except that the speedometer should be housed within a Manx rev-counter-type, anti-vibration housing

Left

Pictured at a pre-war ISDT time-check point, P. Southall of the RAC's trials team. He is riding a near zero-ground-clearance International, precisely why Norton themselves favoured the higher CS1 chassis

Below

No idea who this ES2 rider is, but the bike certainly reminds me of Jack Williams' 1937 Scottish Six Days winner

Below

The ill-fated, prototype, military side-valve twin of 1953 also used a derivative of the 500T's chassis

Right

The standard 500T's unique gearbox end-cover short boss and matching shorter kickstarter shaft, although the spring cover is missing on this example

Dominator twins

History is littered with examples of individual motorcycle manufacturers stealing the march on the opposition with for instance, new items like chain drive, hub brakes, gearboxes and clutches. So it was when Norton introduced their revolutionary Featherbed frames.

The Featherbed's enormous improvement in handling alone long allowed Manx riders to continue thrashing far faster machines, and it led to this type of frame being sought after, or copied, ever since for housing even more powerful or larger engines than ever intended. Furthermore, by introducing this one item on their own 500 cc roadster Dominator, Norton at last made an ordinary bike become 'unapproachable'.

This story really begins in the mid 1940s, however, with Bert Hopwood being recruited from Triumph to design a robust, 500 cc, twin-cylinder engine for slotting into the ES2's existing plunger-rear-suspension frame. On its 1949 début, this was named the Dominator Model 7, due to it having a maximum performance of 77 mph on pool petrol.

The roadholding and handling of these particular bikes, frankly, were anything but good, not least because they shared exactly the same running gear as the equally-poor-steering, single-cylinder job. However, Hopwood's new 500 cc engine soon proved itself an absolute jewel. Indeed, it was so understressed that it grew ever larger over the years, eventually even powering the 850 Commando.

Those home-market Dominators (and ES2s) eventually received a rather heavy swinging-arm rear suspension from September 1951, whereas the export-only versions were unveiled as Dominator 88s with pukka Featherbed frames. The increase from 77 to 88, incidentally, implied an additional 10 mph top speed gained by the new chassis' considerable saving in weight.

Sadly, Britain's motorcyclists had to wait another full year for this bike, and even by 1954, they were still so scarce that I can remember joining a long, impromptu queue that formed outside my local Norton agent, Palins of Derby, after the word that they had one had spread like wildfire. Palins certainly rose to the occasion by persuading the machine's lucky new owner to let them keep it on show for a month.

Half of Derbyshire seemingly came for a drool, yet Norton were in absolutely no position to meet the obvious marketing potential, for the vital Featherbed frames were being hand-built by Reynolds Tubing, who could only manage to supply around 70 each week. The vast majority of those were still equipping machines destined for export.

Welding the tubes together, rather than brazing them, eventually speeded up this process slightly, as did making the rear subframe a permanent fixture, rather than having it as a separate bolted-on unit, which all happened from 1954 onwards. The alloy, instead of cast-iron, cylinder heads for 1955 marked

Right

Not a thoroughbred in the author's view, despite Norton's claims about their 1951 'garden gate' framed Model 7 Dominator, for this bike's handling left much to be desired

72

THE UNAPPROACHABLE

Norton

THE WORLD'S BEST ROAD-HOLDER

Dominator

Built in the light of Experience

WINNER OF 24 T.T. RACES

NORTON MOTORS LIMITED
BRACEBRIDGE STREET BIRMINGHAM·6

Right
Likewise 1951, and the far-superior prototype Featherbed twin, which is now in Sammy Miller's museum

Far right
Mid-1950s 99 with alloy cylinder head and full-width wheel hubs – absolutely oozing quality with good looks

Below
Once, this was my much-loved Dominator 88 of 1954 period – lovely to look at, but those early iron engines were rather slow

the first significant attempt at developing the engines further.

The 68 × 82 mm (instead of 66 × 72.6 mm) bore and stroke, 588 cc Model 99 appeared a year later, when both capacities also received Daytona-type camshafts and quieter-running, wire-wound pistons. The magneto and dynamo were dispensed with for 1958 in favour of Lucas' new crankshaft-mounted, 6 volt, AC generator and coil ignition.

Further tuning developments came thick and fast, following the settling of the Suez crisis, which allowed access to higher-octane fuels. These included twin carburettors, racing-type, stellite-tipped valves, and a 9:1 piston compression ratio as options for 1959, whereas 1960 saw a larger-valved, better-ported, higher-compression-ratio cylinder head, that gave an extra 2 bhp, as standard for both engine capacities.

This was when Norton revised the Featherbed design from its previous

Above

Norton had the occasional habit of taking one step forward, but two back. Witness the 77 for 1957, which used the pre-Featherbed frame and all of the old heavy bits, i.e. it was really a Model 7 except for the alloy cylinder head

Left

The 1957 Featherbeds were cheapened by such items as plastic badges and chrome side plates which were bolted to their fuel tanks. This one is a 99

With slimline frame and different tank badges without any chrome panel surrounds, Dave Catton's superbly-restored 1960 Dominator 99 looks mean and purposeful

'wideline' configuration to 'slimline', which was achieved by substantially crimping the frame's two rear top tubes inwards. This, in turn, allowed for matching reductions in seat and fuel tank widths, greatly benefiting those shorter riders who had had difficulty in touching the ground on the old version.

Mid 1961 brought the additional 88 and 99 SS (Supersport) models, featuring twin carburettors, an extra 40-thou. cam lift, thermal-slot pistons and cylinder heads with increased induction-port downdraught angles. Although initially only for export, these were joined at the year's end by the 745 cc single-carburettor Atlas, plus the really hot 650 SS versions intended for

The metallic grey and white finish for this 1961 SS version is rather drab, but, fortunately, there were other colour options

Rear enclosure became available for the de luxe models, as demonstrated by this 88 of 1961. Lest anyone should be misled by the 'J' suffix on the number plate, John Anderson's 100-per-cent-original bike was stored for 11 years before being registered

Roy Bird's green and cream 1962 twin-carburettor Dominator 88SS, a real beauty

production racing.

The ordinary touring 99s had become virtually superfluous by then, so only four were built in the whole of 1962, and all used the earlier non-downdraught-pattern cylinder heads with small inlet valves, along with coil ignition. However, the sportier and last ever Bracebridge Street-built SS model 'Dommies' reverted to magneto ignition just prior to production being transferred from Birmingham to Associated Motor Cycles at Plumstead in London.

AMC slashed the previously unwieldy range to just five models for 1963, i.e.

the single-carburettor 500, 650 and 750 (the latter still for export only), plus the 88 and 650 SS versions. My own view, although contrary to popular opinion, is that these and all future Nortons greatly benefited from Plumstead's fresh influence on development.

Wally Wyatt, who was AMC's works competition engine guru, took a close look at Norton's powerplants and almost immediately reported on potentially serious lubrication inadequacies. He also stated that the cylinder head's exhaust ports were of very poor design, which was amply backed up by results on the test-bed, where he proved that these engines were wasting much of their undoubted performance potential.

Wyatt recalled: 'You couldn't get your little finger down the exhaust port, it was so crooked. They (Nortons) had done all of that work on the inlet side to get a good petrol/air charge in, then thrown it away again because the exhaust valves couldn't push burnt gases out quickly enough.' Hence, yet another, and this time better-ported, head casting arriving.

The lubrication deficiencies were due to the oil pump having a flow rate which did not match the external supply and return pipe bore sizes, meaning that it spent as much time sucking and blowing air as oil. This was soon cured by fitting six (instead of three) start-work drive pinions, thus, increasing and matching oil delivery.

Dominators and Atlases won numerous world-class road-races, including Silverstone's 1000-Kilometre International Production Race of 1962, along with Thruxton's equally-prestigious 500-miler twice in a row. Furthermore, Rex Butcher took one of Paul Dunstall's 750 cc 'Domiracers' to Monza's concrete bowl during 1967 and smashed BMW's six-year domination of the 1-hour-duration world speed record by averaging 126.7 mph.

Ray Pickrell's Dunstall 'Domiracer' gave Norton their penultimate Isle of Man TT victory in 1968 by winning the 750 cc Production Race at 98.13 mph; similarly-mounted Billie Nelson finished second. Paul Smart took the runner-up spot in 1967 and 1969, although on the latter occasion, his bike was virtually a Commando.

All of these models are comparatively rare nowadays because Norton never could make enough to go around in the first place. Moreover, many were broken up to build specials based on the fabulous-handling Featherbed chassis, usually with Triumph or 1000 cc Vincent powerplants. Although once a very fashionable dodge, in retrospect, this seems more than a pity.

Ironically, there was nothing really wrong with Norton's own engines. Indeed, the SS and later 650 cc versions were arguably always better than most of their popular replacements. Therefore, my personal 'Dommie' favourites are the 1953–5 era versions for fabulous looks, and those final and less fussy 650 cc, single-carburettor, (American-market Mercury) tourers for all-round comfort allied to stunning performance.

Most of the twin-carburettor 'Dommies' tended to vibrate somewhat, while the mighty Atlas, although only having a single carb, is quite capable of

Left
Ian Verrinder's bike looks much the same as Roy Bird's, but, in fact, is a 750 Atlas of 1965 vintage

shaking out all of one's dental fillings on a long run. This, of course, is why NVT's Bernard Hooper eventually mounted this engine on rubber for the Commando, but more on that in a later chapter.

Left

The highly-tuned, twin-carburettor 650SS was faster and vibrated less than the Atlas, while enjoying a much lower seat height than the Commando. It is my favourite twin-cylinder Norton of all

Below

The green 'blobs' on this 1969 American-spec. Mercury's instruments illustrate that it overlapped Norton-Villiers' Commando, so it was already on borrowed time

Jubilees and Navigators

Rather than 1959's ill-fated twin-cylinder Jubilee, Norton had actually intended producing a 250 cc single-cylinder machine, as designed by Jackie Moore during the very early 1950s. This model's sporty little unit-construction engine closely followed Vincent-HRD practice, having similar high camshafts, transverse rocker arms and widely-splayed pushrods, etc.

The duplex chassis used was virtually a mini Featherbed, and Chris Vincent, the famous sidecar racer who did most of the 1954 prototype's road testing, reported that it would hold 80 mph, two-up, uphill or down. In those days, such performance must have suggested a TT racing potential.

Only one prototype and a spare engine were built before it came to the attention of Norton's London-based (AMC) bosses, who promptly demanded that everything be destroyed. It seems that they were not prepared to risk this exciting new bike posing a threat to their own lacklustre James and Francis Barnett lightweights.

Bob Collier was handed a sledgehammer and given the unenviable task of destruction. Years later, he recalled, with some considerable mirth, that the complete bike disappeared before he could attack it, and of the engine: 'They stood over me as I raised the sledgehammer, but I was careful not to let it drop too forcefully, and when the gaffers' backs were turned I salvaged it.'

Sadly, Bob passed away in 1990, but due to his efforts, that engine survived, complete with dents from the sledgehammer. It is on show now as part of Sammy Miller's famous collection, whereas the complete bike turned up years later, likewise via Bob Collier, and can be seen in the National Motorcycle Museum.

In fact, such new product designs, and even major revamps, were rare occurrences at Bracebridge Street, primarily because they never had the necessary machinery to cope. What few mills, lathes and jig borers they did have were usually Shelley Group cast-offs, i.e. long past their best when Norton first received them.

With these limitations in mind, Norton needed to keep their design strategy simple, preferably while avoiding any fine-tolerance, multi-machining operations which might have cost them a fortune in rejects. It also meant that Bracebridge Street's men were virtually obliged to get every detail component right in the first place, for it was unlikely that they would be revised.

There were some exceptions, however, including the famous racing Manx, for which heaven and earth could always be moved. Others were the Bert Hopwood-inspired Jubilee and Navigator twins, whose engines proved decidedly complex to manufacture compared to Jackie Moore's design, and hence cost a small fortune when it came to sorting the multitude of ensuing guarantee claims.

Right
Jackie Moore's ill-fated (and dented), high-cam, 250 cc single engine, now displayed in Sammy Miller's museum

NORTON 250 cc

EXPERIMENTAL
PROTOTYPE ENGINE

NEVER PRODUCED

Terry Brocks' fully-restored 1961 Jubilee certainly looks nice, but...

More cubes and a superior front end on Chris Davis' 1961 Navigator, which had only covered 45,000 miles from new when this photo was taken

'Pa' Norton must have turned in his grave when AMC changed their previous policy and, in 1959, unveiled a Francis Barnett Cruiser 80 fitted with this latter oil-leaking, gutless, over-square (60 × 44 mm), 250 cc parallel twin engine. He had even more reason to do so when they christened the Norton Jubilee in honour of the 60th anniversary of his founding of the company!

Frankly, there is little favourable to be said of these grossly under-braked 250 cc machines which, at 340 lb wet, were far too heavy for the engine's 16 bhp maximum (Triumph's 199 cc Cub offered 14.5 bhp to push a bike weighing over 100 lb less). Having broken with the 'keep it simple' edict, these Jubilees were beset from their outset with numerous mechanical problems.

Perhaps fortunately, they never did sell in large numbers, and neither, sadly, would the much-improved, longer-stroke, 350 cc Navigators of 1960 onwards. This was despite the fact that Norton's own infinitely-superior front

forks and brake were fitted, and that they enjoyed a 6 bhp power increase (to 22 bhp) to propel much the same overall weight as their predecessors.

Best versions of all were the 1963-onwards Electras, whose electric-start engines were overbored by yet another 3 mm to 383 cc and which also came with a decent rear brake to match that of the front. Collectively, they became a very nice package, yet none the less, one which was never able to outlive the justly deserved poor reputation of the Jubilee base model.

The greatest pity was that all of these models might have been so much better, and reasonably successful in the market place, if Bracebridge Street had been given some decent manufacturing machinery, and perhaps even more so if Hopwood's original engine design had been left well alone. Unfortunately, however, he had left so the bikes were revised by a committee before any of them reached fruition.

January 1963, by which time Navigator production was in full swing at AMC's Plumstead factory rather than at Bracebridge Street in Birmingham

Left

Henry Dulat's very original Electra seen from the other side

Far left

Timing-side of Henry Dulat's Electra, showing the electric starter motor. This was exactly the same, incidentally, as those fitted to Mk 3 Commandos

Left

Most of the survivors? A gaggle of Navigators, Jubilees and Electras seen at the Norton Owners' Club's 1990 International Rally. Furthermore, most of these arrived and left under their own steam

Above

Eighty-five quid with log book, and no doubt prepared to haggle. That just about sums up the autojumble fate of most Jubilees

Commandos galore

Dennis Poore's Manganese Bronze Group's 1966 rescue of Associated Motor Cycles followed their mix-and-match period of asset stripping, during which, for instance, the Atlas engine found its way into inferior AJS and Matchless chassis components, and surplus pre-Featherbed frames were used in the final AMC-powered Nortons.

To us outsiders, not knowing that AMC were about to go bankrupt, none of these machines made much sense at the time. They could no longer afford to pay Reynolds Tubing to provide Featherbed frames, so were reduced to raiding their own stores and building these decidedly parts-bin specials in an attempt to stay alive.

AMC's residue, and the Villiers engine manufacturers, Manganese Bronze, were reconstituted as Norton-Villiers after the crash. For a while, this exercise continued with such Atlas-engined machines as Norton's P11 and the Matchless G15C, etc. Then, out of the blue, during September 1967, they announced the almost all-new Commando.

The main frame of this revolutionary machine bore no relationship whatsoever to its proven Featherbed predecessor, for the 750 cc Atlas power unit had the entire rear swinging fork and wheel assembly attached directly to the engine and gearbox. These, in turn, were hung from a massively-spined, but ultra-light, main frame, fabricated from Reynolds' famous 531 tubing. The power unit's mountings were vibration-absorbing, metal-to-rubber 'isolastic' fittings.

Weighing in at a mere 398 lb, this was genuinely the fastest and most powerful production machine in the world and, incidentally, one which could be supplied 'ex-factory' with any of Paul Dunstall's three-stage production race tuning kits. These would turn the already 120 mph base model roadsters instantly into 140 mph missiles.

Less well thought of, however, were the plain plastic, roundel fuel tank and rear mudguard badges, with nothing, not even the Norton legend, written on them. Despite the enormous demand for these models, the badges usually caused them to be known irreverently as Dennis' 'green blobs'. However, the overall build quality was very high.

Bernard Hooper's rubber-mounting idea solved the Atlas engine's previous vibration problems at a stroke, for now it could shake away merrily without any real signs of stress ever reaching the rider. Furthermore, an all-new diaphragm-type clutch, coupled to far heavier-duty drive chains, provided an effective means of putting the excess of power on the road.

Production moved from the old Plumstead AMC factory to Andover, in Wiltshire, during 1969, when the new 'Yellow Peril' production racer and Norton's Interpol police model first went on sale. Then a whole series of relatively minor restyling exercises resulted in the larger fuel-tanked

Interstates, and the 1973-onwards, larger-capacity 850 engines.

The latter came about by increasing the bore of the previously 73 × 89 mm, 749 cc engine to 77 mm, which actually gave 829 and not 850 cc, but no one much minded the deception. However, there has always been disagreement among *aficionados* as to which size of engine is best, my own favourites being the stronger and more torquey early 850s, the top speed of which, incidentally, remained much as before.

Later Commandos suffered increasingly from restrictions brought about by America's introduction of lead-free petrol and their exhaust-emission controls, for by this time, Norton could no longer afford to build separate versions.

The fabulous P11 prototype for 1967 used the Rickman-devised Matchless G85CS, World Championship-winning motocross chassis and Norton's meaty 750 cc engine. What a pity that it never reached full production.

Above

*Atlanta, Georgia, and the production P11
on show. It used the older and far-heavier
Matchless G80-type frame for its Atlas
engine, so was but a poor relation to the
gorgeous prototype*

Right

*An early 750 Commando, but already
fitted with second-generation tank badges*

Thus, 1974's unrestricted 850 Mk IIAs are arguably best of all, the more so
because they had not yet been saddled with the Mk III's needlessly-heavy,
though useless, electric-start system.

Peter Williams and Mick Grant used works-prepared versions of the earlier-
type engines to finish first and second in 1973's Formula 750 TT, sadly, the
Commando's only Isle of Man victory, despite numerous near misses. This win
proved to be Norton's last, some 66 years after Rem Fowler gave them their
first. The final 30 of an estimated 60–80,000 production Commandos rolled off
Andover's assembly lines in early 1978.

Many of this total are still in regular use, and even by today's standards are
reasonably fast, while being quite capable over twisting roads of out-handling
all but the very latest superbikes. However, the brakes are of yesteryear's

technology, and the bottom-gear ratio is just a little too high for really enjoyable riding in modern stop-start traffic conditions.

Spares availability remains excellent, Norton themselves now remanufacturing components. Moreover, these twins' rather lumpy power delivery can be smoothed out enormously by spending half an hour or so fitting one of the surprisingly-cheap, and simple, proprietary electronic

Far left
Mike Gower and his beautifully-kept 1971 Fastback

Overleaf
Other than changing the twistgrip rubbers to ones he preferred, Mike Gower has kept his one-owner bike just as it was when he bought it new

Left
No excuses for using a third 1971 Fastback picture, for this model was arguably best of them all

Left
Pilot's eye view of a Dunstall-modified
Fastback, which came with all of the
official go-faster goodies

Above
Looking gorgeous, a 1971 Dunstall
Fastback. As I recall, however, these
models' seats were as hard as the
proverbial boards

ignition kits in place of Joe Lucas' original, crude, separate points system.

Earlier models also benefit greatly from discarding their engine mountings in favour of the later Mk 3's components, which are more efficient, longer-lasting and easier to adjust. Furthermore, all of these bikes' brakes can be dramatically improved by either fitting a double-disc front-end conversion or, equally, the Norvil racing-type stopper.

Both options are available currently, but prove rather expensive due to the need to change the lower fork sliders as well (although the cost of a life is not particularly cheap either). Joining the Norton Owners' Club, who offer a discounted, genuine spares availability, plus access to many more like-minded enthusiasts, must always be a worthwhile investment.

Left
Not quite standard, but one of Norton's early production racing replicas, which preceded the pukka 'Yellow Peril' racers

Below
Paul Thomas' Mk 3 electric-start Interstate looks as good as new, but it had endured over 100,000 miles of hard police use before he restored it

Left

Peter Williams gunning the works 750 John Player Special during 1973's Race of the Year

Far left

The roadster model nearest the camera used a smaller fuel tank that also allowed the seat to be fitted further forward. This resulted in a far more comfortable riding position than that provided by the Interstate seen behind

Below

Norton produced around 250 JPS racer look-alikes during 1974. Although highly collectable nowadays, in truth, they were little more than restyled 850 Mk 2A roadsters

Previous page
'Pegasus', the famous and fabulous, dual-engined, supercharged sprinter

Above
Cyril Malen recently gave one of Norton's ex-works Challenge racers a demonstration blast round the Isle of Man TT course

Works rider Dave Croxford during the 1976 Transatlantic Races on the very advanced Cosworth Challenge prototype model. Sadly, this was its one-and-only outing in anger before the money ran out

Rotary revival

As motorcycle manufacturers, Norton gradually rose from the dead by building some 2–300 aircooled, rotary-engined Interpol models exclusively for use by the police, motoring organizations and the military between 1983 and 1987, which is when Phillipe Le Roux headed the most recent takeover. He declared that these interesting bikes would be going public.

The rotary's story began, however, with Fred Umpleby, an inventor from Yorkshire, who originally devised, built and actually patented the world's first working trochoidal engine in 1909. An example of this engine, incidentally, can be seen in his local museum at Keighley, and it bears a remarkable physical resemblance to Dr Felix Wankel's 1950s invention.

Obviously, Umpleby built his version without the aid of modern ceramics, so he never found a really effective, long-lasting method of gas sealing his engine's single rotor which was subject to three explosions per revolution. For that matter, neither had Wankel when he applied for his own patents at almost the very moment that Umpleby expired some 50 years later!

Wankel worked in close collaboration with the German automotive giant, NSU (now part of VW-Audi), and after their prototype RO80 motor car appeared, he announced an interest in selling the rights to his rotary during 1959 to other manufacturers, on the basis of welcoming bids from any motorcycle or car producer from each interested country.

Amazingly, this sparked off a Dutch auction during the early 1960s, leading to a period of Wankel mania. Many giants, including Suzuki, Mazda, Sachs, DKW and BSA, hastily staked vast sums rather than risk being outbid by their opposition. Most of those who survived the ensuing huge development costs were to repent at their leisure.

BSA, Suzuki and DKW virtually bankrupted themselves trying to solve the same rotor/housing gas-sealing problems that had defeated Fred Umpleby. Before finally going bust, however, BSA/Triumph managed to partially develop a much superior twin-rotor engine which, in a spare Triumph chassis, produced a machine that weighed a mere 328 lb and offered 125 mph maximum with shattering acceleration.

This engine was inherited by Dennis Poore's Manganese Bronze Group. The Group had become Norton-Villiers-Triumph (NVT) when Britain's government offered a £4.8 million inducement to persuade them to attempt salvaging something from the collapsing industry's latest victims – BSA/Triumph.

Poore readily accepted the taxpayers' millions because he wanted BSA/Triumph's well-proven, triple-cylinder (Trident) powerplant, which he saw as the obvious replacement for his own company's Commando engine, the design of which went back nigh on a quarter of a century. However, this option was effectively denied him when Triumph's workforce commenced

their famous sit-in at Meriden.

Events dragged on for several years before Meriden's occupying forces were offered yet another large donation of government money to set up on their own. The terms of this arrangement also obliged NVT to hand back all of the former BSA/Triumph Group's remaining assets to Meriden, that is except the rotary which, apparently, neither side much wanted.

Further ministerial interference precluded NVT from selling or making anything else but motorcycles, unless they also repaid the £4.8 million, which had been proffered, remember, to persuade the purchase of the very assets that Poore had to give away. As events turned out, this finally broke the camel's back.

NVT's bankruptcy followed almost automatically, although the most famous name in motorcycling was saved by Poore, who set up today's relatively tiny Norton Motors Company at Shenstone. With no other engine

Above
Trevor Nation spearheading Norton's racing comeback at 1988's Isle of Man Senior TT – last-lap engine problems robbed him of 12th place

Left
Note the eventual production Classic's slightly different seat and side-panel lines compared to the prototype

*Simon Buckmaster was lured away from
500 cc Grand Prix racing to campaign
Norton's 1988 F1 bike, although
unfortunately, it proved a mutually
unhappy liaison*

designs to choose from, the company spent the ten followng years quietly
perfecting the forgotten Wankel.

Early in 1987, Le Roux's City-backed consortium took over Norton and by
that December announced that they would be offering a limited production
run of 1000 civilian Classic aircooled, rotary-engined machines. These were to
be painted in Norton's traditional black and silver colours, hopefully to tempt
some of the wealthier collectors to part with a then staggering £5700.

Such optimism certainly proved justified, for every one of those 83 bhp
machines was spoken for within the following three weeks. This was despite
the fact that it was fairly general knowledge that the near identical engines in
British police service were suffering incurable carburation problems, and that
Norton had admitted to having a superior, watercooled replacement waiting in
the wings.

The 588 cc (nominal) Classic and police models – tested at 125.2 mph,
incidentally, with the rider seated normally – literally drank petrol. This was

because their two $1\frac{1}{2}$ in. SU constant-velocity carburettors were fed with air which had passed through the engine to cool its internal rotors. Consequently, it had already become far too hot for any hope of truly efficient carburation or fuel mixing.

Only 1000 were to be made because Norton were well on the way towards producing the watercooled replacement, which would not suffer these carburation glitches. In the meantime, however, Le Roux had decided that Norton should re-enter racing after an RC88, tuned and ridden by Malcolm Heath, had touched speeds well in excess of 170 mph at the Motor Industry Research Association's test track.

Success for the resulting 135 bhp racer came amazingly quickly, Steve Spray literally smashing Japan's mega-buck opposition to win 1989's UK Formula One Championship. Then his team-mate, Trevor Nation, rekindled hopes of renewing Norton's Isle of Man glory when he finished a remarkably close second in 1990's Senior TT.

Buckmaster's replacement, Steve Spray, finally made the big breakthrough when he broke Japan's long-held dominance and easily won 1989's British F1 Championship outright with this watercooled rotary

A sight for sore eyes: Trevor Nation and Norton rotary on the front row of the grid, Donington Park, 1989

Left

Lap record holder Steve Cull was drafted into Norton's 1989 TT line-up and he is seen here blasting off in the World Championship-counting F1 race

Above

One might wish that this was all the opposition saw of Steve Cull in 1989's Senior TT, but his Norton's engine blew on the last lap, leaving him with a long uphill push just to finish in lowly 23rd place

That same year also saw the launch of the new watercooled, fully faired, and ready panniered Commander, which was based on the police Interpol model and similarly offered 85 bhp with almost uncanny smoothness. There was also the phenomenally-expensive, racer-based F1 Sports Roadster, whose 93.7 bhp is quite sufficient to propel this bike to a very illegal 155 mph in mere seconds before its rev limiter cuts in at 10,500 rpm.

Le Roux claimed, 'This is the Porsche of motorcycles'. Sadly, the £12,700 F1's 'Made in Britain' content is rather limited, for gearboxes, carburettors and instruments are all Japanese, the brakes are Italian Brembo, the suspension is Swedish White Power, and the tyres are French Michelin. Undoubtedly, however, Norton now leads the world in rotary-engine technology.

Norton's fully-faired, watercooled Commander tourer was introduced for 1990 in any colour you liked, as long as it was dark metallic grey. That did not please owner Steve Medlin, seen here

Steve Medlin took a can of BMW metallic paint to Norton when ordering his Commander, and the result was so nice that they now offer this colour and metallic blue as options

Right
Trevor Nation fighting tooth and nail to give Norton's slightly-off-the-pace rotary a 1990 Senior TT win; he finished a truly brilliant second and was looking forward to 1991

Below
Nice bike, shame about the colour – the new F1 Sportster model as it finally entered production midway through 1990